BUDGET BUDDY

ANGELA FRANCIS-PHILLIPS

AllocatedFunds

Stone Mountain, GA

BUDGET BUDDY: INTERACTIVE WORKBOOK
©2019 Angela Francis-Phillips

For more information, contact the publisher:

Allocated Funds
www.allocatedfunds.com

ISBN: 978-0-578-45247-0

Cover Design: Paper Trail
Illustrations: Osman Martinez

First Printing December 2018

Printed in the United States of America

THIS BOOK BELONGS TO

_____

YOUR NAME HERE

DEDICATION

To everyone—no one deserves to spend their life in debt. Financial freedom is for everyone and can be achieved by anyone that is willing to discipline themselves with a budget, long enough to experience the change. No matter what you make, you can still live the life you want when you get control of your money. Paul Clitheroe said it best, *"The amount of money you have has got nothing to do with what you earn. People earning a million dollars a year can have no money. People earning $35,000 a year can be quite well off. It's not what you earn, it's what you spend."*

TABLE OF CONTENTS

W.H.Y.—WHY HELP YOURSELF

"Those who have a strong enough why, can bear almost any now."
~F. Nietzsche

BUDGET—the word often makes people cringe. It could be because it requires one to say "no" to the things they want. It could be because it requires one to put more energy towards saying "yes" to what they need. It could be simply because no one really wants to be reined in from doing what they want to do with the money that they work so hard for. No matter what the "because" is, in order for financial security to be achieved and maintained, budgeting is a principal that has to be implemented into one's daily life.

So, let's clear up the misconceptions. The first one being that a budget is: not spending money on the things you want at all until you get what it is you need to get it. That is not true! **Budgeting is a limitation plan to manage your personal money**. The limitation is not to be confused with stagnation. Limits within budgeting allows for you to prioritize what is important and what is not so important. Budgets also help you to see where it is that most of your money is being spent. Another misconception is: budgets only work for those that have a lot of money. This is an absolute lie! Budgets can work for anyone that has money coming in. Mind you, if you have more money coming in, then you have more to work with and build with. But anyone—anyone, can budget!

You have to have a job, or some means of regular income coming in, but yes, a budget can be established for the person working for $8.00 an hour, to the C.F.O making over 100k annually. The last misconception that I want to touch on is: you only have to budget if you are trying to make a big purchase. What! Please do not believe that. Budgets are great if you are working towards the purchase of a home or a car, an engagement ring for that special girl or the trip of a lifetime. However, if you established a budget prior to making those types of purchases, you will be in better financial standing when you make them. Get it? Got it? Good!

Now that you have a clearer understanding of what budgeting isn't, let's talk more about what it is. Budgeting is the analysis of one's income and expense finances. It is the managing of the monies coming in, so that you can better control the monies going out. It is the "now" decision that helps you in the "soon to come" financial decisions. It benefits you in the long run so that you can live your best life. It prepares you for the future you desire.

I know. I know. You have been doing pretty good in life so far. You have been able to maintain and sustain life with the money you make. But who wants to just be okay? Don't you know that you are made to prosper, and that more than enough is your assigned portion? Implementing a budget in your daily life is a way to help yourself. **Why Help Yourself—why?** Simply because there is no such things as too much good help. Keep this in mind, "the plan of the diligent lead to profit as surely as haste leads to poverty."

If you have people depending on you, or a business venture you're trying to fund, or a home, car or wedding you're wanting to pay for, or even a debt that you are tired of looking at–you could use help. Any of those previously mentioned reasons could be an answer to your why!

Now, I have been doing this for years, so I do understand that some people don't start off with a clear why at all. So, let's jump in to one of several assignments you have to complete in this workbook, starting with the question, what is your why?

Get out your pencil. Answer the following questions by circling yes or no. No one is looking over your shoulder, so answer the questions honestly.

1. Yes or No: Was this workbook given to you by someone?

2. Yes or No: Do you care to know about budgeting, why it's important, and how it can help you?

3. Yes or No: Do you need help with managing your money?

4. Yes or No: Are you ready to see a change in your finances for the better?

5. Yes or No: Are you ready to make the necessary changes to shift your finances for the

better. If no, why not? _____

_____

_____

_____

_____

_____

6. Yes or No: Can you list every area in which you spend money—i.e. church, food, bills, etc.?

_____

_____

_____

7. Yes or No: Do you feel overwhelmed by the line of questioning thus far? If so, why?

_____

_____

_____

_____

_____

Short Response: Answer the following questions in detail on the corresponding lines.

8. What are 3 of financial goals that you deem most important to accomplish?

_____

_____

_____

_____

9. Where is most of your money being spent and why?

_____

_____

_____

_____

_____

_____

I can hear it now. Your future is thanking you for taking the first step to financial responsibility and financial security. But the interrogation is not done yet. Here's just a few more questions for ya!

Grab that pencil, and answer the following questions by circling yes or no.

10. Yes or No: Do you have a checking account?

11. Yes or No: Do you have a savings account?

12. Yes or No: Do you have a prepaid debit card?

13. Yes or No: Do you often borrow money from family/friends?

14. Yes or No: Do you owe money in any amount to bill collectors/family/friends?

If you've answered "yes" to any of those questions, then this workbook is for you, and will be a best friend to you. Completing this first questionnaire shows that you are ready for the push that will properly position you into a secure financial future.

MONEY MENTALITY

"Don't tell me what you value, show me your budget, and it'll tell you what you value."
~Joe Biden

HOW do you look at money? Your truth about this question can either make or break the shift that will take place in your finances. Money is not a bad thing. It is dirty because everyone touches it, but money does answer *all* things, and I'm certain that you have lots of questions.

Coming to terms on how you feel about money, and your thoughts about money will make all the difference because perception is everything. No one is born with poor money management habits, but you can be taught poor money management habit—consciously or subconsciously. Money management habits are passed down based on what you've seen growing up. For example, maybe you've always seen your parents dodge the bill collectors, or had the car repossessed. You may have friends that shop more than they save. All these factors subconsciously frame the mental workings of your "money mind".

Hey! Now, I'm not saying that everything you saw growing up was bad. Maybe you grew up sitting at the table while your parents reconciled their check books. You may have heard them make payment arrangements with collectors. Maybe your friends shopped less, but still didn't save. Who knows but you. Those factors are better, but you have to consider—were the payment arrangements met and met on time? Were your parents stressed out when they were reconciling the check books? How many family vacations or wants were you all able to indulge in?

Growing up, if you've had or seen more negative or inconsistent money management habits, chances are that you have grown up not to manage money as best as you should—if at all. But, do not get mad and please do not be discouraged. This is not geared towards offending you. If anything, it is a mirror that you have no choice but to look in to in order to get to where you need to be. You may not even think or care that you have a poor money mindset, but you should.

Trust me when I say that I know financial obligations and financial setbacks are a part of life. It happens to the best of us, even those that have tons of money. Now is the time–the time is now to get a handle on it! Do not panic. Take a breather and keep moving forward. You are doing what you have to do so that you can do what you want to do. It's all about shifting your mindset.

It's time for that pencil again! Here are a few more questions. This time they are focused on your perception of money. Answer the following questions by circling yes or no. Again, no one is looking over your shoulder, so answer honestly.

1. Yes or No: Are you ready to live your best life?

2. Yes or No: Are you afraid to see where your money is going?

3. Yes or No: Are you a visual person that needs to physically see the budget?

Short Response: Answer the following questions in detail on the corresponding lines.

4. My definition of money is:

_____

_____

_____

_____

_____

5. Money makes me feel: _____

    because _____

6. What do you use to track the money you spend, and why?

_____

_____

_____

_____

_____

_____

_____

CASH FLOW

"It always come down to money. The biggest problem is juggling the cash flow."

~Dan Wyam

I
T IS said that in order for one to know where they're going they must first know where they've been. This is true when it comes to finances as well. Knowing your cash flow will help you differentiate between what bills are fixed and which are fluctuating. **Fixed bills are those that are regular with a guaranteed number**. The cost barely or never changes at all. **Fluctuating bills are those with numerical figures that change regularly**. For example, your cellphone bill could be fixed, but your transportation bills may be fluctuating.

At the end of the day, you need to know what your bills are. **Bills are any and all monies that are paid out for any reason**. This means any money that you pay to bills, business or yourself. Do yourself and your future a favor–complete the following chart by circling all that applies. It's time to find out what's coming in and why it's going out!

On the chart below, circle the items that describe what avenues your money is coming from.

INCOMING CASH FLOW CHART			
Full-Time Salary	Monthly Salary	Weekly Salary	Semi-Monthly Salary
Part-Time Salary	Child Support	Social Security	Disability
Alimony	State Assistance	Govt. Assistance	Side Hustle
Personal Business	Allowances	2nd/3rd Job	Family Assistance

Now that you have a better scope of where your money is coming in from, let's take a look at where your money is going. If you haven't been honest in any other point of this workbook, this is the area that you should be. It's the only way for you to experience true financial gain.

On the chart below, circle the avenues that your money is being allocated to.

OUTGOING CASH FLOW CHART			
Rent	Trash	Hulu	Car Insurance
Mortgage	Student Loans	Internet	Car Note
Utility/Gas Bill	Cable	Cellphone	Health Insurance (outside of job)
Water Bill	Netflix	Business Expenses	Life Insurance
Child Care	Public Transportation	Uber/Lyft	Lessons
Savings Account	Credit Cards	Groceries	Eating Out
Tithing	Paying Debt (Family/Friends)	Church Contributions	Clothing
Bowling	Clubbing	Date Night	Gym Membership
Spotify/Apple Music	Gas (Car)	Makeup	Manicure/Pedicure
Hair Care	Massages	Child Support	Movies
Collections Agency	Staycations	Vacations	Random Acts of Kindness
Car Wash	Shoes	Medical Bills	Doctor Visits

This is great! You are on the right track. If anything, you should have better insight to what you bring in and what you are shelling out monetarily. You finally see all your bills at a closer view. If you did this right you probably sat there circling lots of categories and asking yourself "why am I paying for this, can I do without this, or why am I spending in these areas?"

There are things that are unnecessary, which you can change. There are things that can be reduced, things that can be paid off and things that are considered normal financial obligations, for example, rent or mortgage. There is room for improvement for everyone, and it can be done. Properly allocating your funds sets you up for success.

Let's take it a step further. From the incoming cash flow chart, list each stream of income you have on the lines below, then write the amount that stream brings in. Estimates are okay, but to reap the true benefit of establishing your budget, an accurate number is recommended.

1. _____

2. _____

3. _____

4. _____

5. _____

6. _____

7. _____

8. _____

9. _____

10. _____

11. _____

12. _____

13. _____

14. _____

15. _____

16. _____

If you notice self –categories were added—nails, hair, clothes, et cetera. You have to put money aside for these items. After all, when one looks their best they feel their best, and budgets are designed to help you live your best life, not make you feel like your best life has to be on hold. If anything, you'll live your best life on your current level, until you are placed in a position to level up. Personal care should be considered a bill. Most financial advisors classify those type of expenses as miscellaneous, but they're not. They are a factor in your spending. However, they should not be the largest factor of your spending. Setting a budget will most definitely put you in a position where you can get your hair and nails done, but you may not be able to do that every pay period.

We're still moving! From the outgoing cash flow chart, list each avenue that you spend money by writing it on the lines below with the amount that you pay out. Again, estimates are okay, but to reap the true benefit of establishing your budget, an accurate number is recommended. Now, you have 45 lines, but I am hoping that you aren't spending money in all these areas.

1. _____

2. _____

3. _____

4. _____

5. _____

6. _____

7. _____

8. _____

9. _____

10. _____

11. _____

12. _____

13. _____

14. _____

15. _____

16. _____

17. _____

18. _____

19. _____

20. _____

21. _____

22. _____

23. _____

24. _____

25. _____

26. _____

27. _____

28. _____

29. _____

30. _____

31. _____

32. _____

33. _____

34. _____

35. _____

36. _____

37. _____

38. _____

39. _____

40. _____

41. _____

42. _____

43. _____

44. _____

45. _____

PAST DUE BILLS

"A man in debt is so far a slave."
~ Ralph Waldo Emerson

JUST because you don't pay or want to pay a bill does not make it irrelevant. Out of sight, out of mind is not how bills work. I'm sure that you know as well as I do that bill collectors care nothing about your feelings behind the bills they've sent you. Any bill that you have that you don't want to pay that the due date has already passed, it is past due.

Past due bills are not where you want to be, but if you are, proper budgeting will help get you caught up. Remember in the first chapter we talked about your financial goals. In order to get to that goal, you have to eliminate all the hurdles—even if you're the one that set them up.

Pencil time! Answer these questions as honestly and clearly as you can. Circle yes or no to answer.

1. Yes or No: Are you behind on any bill?

2. Yes or No: Do you have bills that are recently past due–30 days or less?

3. Yes or No: Do you have credit card, medical, utility, or collection debts?

4. Yes or No: Have you made payment arrangements for any of your past due bills?

5. Yes or No: Have you been consistent with paying the arrangement(s)?

6. Yes or No: Does your past due bills accrue late fees?

7. Yes or No: You have called and attempted to have a late fee waived?

Short Response: Answer the following questions in detail on the corresponding lines.

8. What bill—not bill(s)...but which bill do you want to payoff first and why?

_____

_____

_____

_____

_____

_____

9. What bills are currently past due? What are the amounts owed? What are the fees, if any?

_____

_____

_____

_____

_____

_____

_____

10. What are the names of the collection agencies that you've contacted? What are the arrangements that were made?

_____

_____

_____

_____

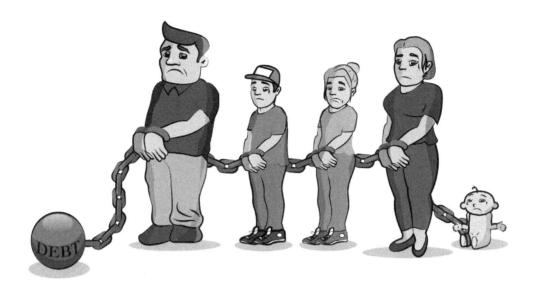

Can I be honest? Most people hate the subject of past due bills. It brings about a sense of shame and at times insecurities. It is one of the hardest parts to face in the budgeting process and where most people tend to become defeated. To you I saw "do not give up!" This is the part of the journey where you have to do what you have to do in order to do what you want to do.

You do not have to be defeated by past due bills. Here's a free tip: one quick way to alleviate the pressure of past due bills is contacting the company and asking them to waive the late fee. Now, this is not a guaranteed strategy. It only works if it is your first time—sorry! If you have overused your waivers, the next step is to begin tackling the payback factor of past due bills with any extra monies you have after your non-negotiable bills are paid.

Every bill you have does not classify as a non-negotiable bill. Clothing, shoes, massages, etc. do not fall under non-negotiables, rent, car note, and insurances are some that do. You can take the extra $10, $40 or $100 towards paying those past due bills. It may not be much, but it is a start. Think about it!

TASK LIST

"When bills come due, only cash is legal tender. Don't leave home without it."

~Warren Buffet

BILLS never stop coming in. It seems like there are more bills than money most times. So, let's get into the nitty gritty of it all. You now know what money comes in, where it goes to, and why. We are getting closer to officially setting your budget.

Let's go to work! You may need to grab a few things besides the pencil, such as your pay stub and gas receipts. If you have direct deposit, then simply use your banking app to fill out this section.

1. My check amount before deductions $_____

2. My check amount after deductions $_____

3. I get paid on_____

4. Based on your pay date and amount after deductions, do you have enough to cover the bills due between the 1st & the 15th? _____

5. Yes or No: Did you add gas into your bills for the 1st half of the month?

6. How much does it take to fill your gas tank? _____

7. How often do you have to refill? _____

On the following chart, list the bills along with the amount and date that are due between the 1st and the 15th of the month. Once you've listed them, add them up and jot down the total.

1st Half of the Month: Bills Due			
Car Note: Toyota 2nd monthly $582.16			
		TOTAL	
2nd Half of the Month: Bills Due			
		TOTAL	
(check – gas – totals=) MONIES LEFT			

It is important to complete both halves of the month. This will help you to see what you have to save and what you have left to pay off debt with. Now, don't pull your hair out because of that "d" word. We'll tackle that in the chapters ahead. But for now, there's a blank calendar that you can fill out based on the month you are charting. Number the days accordingly, list the bills due and the amounts.

Month						
Sunday	Monday	Tuesday	Wednesday	Thursday	Friday	Saturday
					TOTAL	

With your task list complete, you now have your first draft of your budget. Any extra money you have once the task list is complete is to be allocated to your past due bills. Yes! It is not what you wanted to hear. You were probably expecting to hear "go to the mall. Buy something nice because you've done well so far." Nope! You are not to let the start stop you!

You may very well be disheartened. Either you want to go shopping or find that you have very little left to do anything with. Whatever the case is, don't get down. If you don't have much left over, it's okay. Still put what you have to the past due bills. On the next pay cycle, you will add your leftover monies to what you saved prior. This process is to be repeated each pay cycle.

Here is food for thought: "if your bills are consistently exceeding your income, it is time for you to find supplemental income to eliminate unnecessary debt so that you can be stress free and financially successful." It doesn't have to be a permanent resolve, just a temporary fix to get you through to the success that you want.

NEEDS vs. WANTS

"It's not an issue of wants versus needs, but of wants versus priorities."
—Jamie Munson

THOSE with a poor money mind have a blurred line or two when it comes to this concept. Believe it or not, needs and wants are two different things. In the mind of poor money managers, wants and needs comingle because to them everything is important. Such fallacy! The easiest way to separate the two is to determine what is a priority. And, before you say everything is important—lies!

Most that have blurred vision in this area are those that usually have spending issues. Let's see if you are one with a spending issue. Get the pencil out.

Answer these questions as honestly and clearly as you can. Circle yes or no to answer.

1. Yes or No: Do you have a spending problem?

2. Yes or No: Do you spend money when you are stressed as a way to calm you or put your nerves at ease?

3. Yes or No: When you are very happy, do you go shopping/out to eat/vacationing?

4. Yes or No: Does your unintentional spending have you spending beyond your means?

5. Yes or No: Can you do without an unintentional purchase until later?

6. Yes or No: Do you see any areas where you can save a little or a lot?

Short Response: Answer the following questions in detail on the corresponding lines.

7. What is it that you spend the most unintentional money on, i.e. food, sweets, clothes, shoes, vacations, electronics, etc.? Why do you think that is?

_____

_____

_____

_____

Priorities are those things that if left unpaid it will negatively affect your living. For example, if you don't pay your rent you will be put out. If you don't put gas in your car, you won't be able to get to work or where ever you need to go. What you consider to be a need may very well be a want. Take a minute and flip back to your task list. Is there anything that you listed as a bill that you can avoid paying? Are you willing to eliminate them for the moment or forever? List them on the chart below along with the amount.

Bill Eliminator	

CREDIT CARDS

THOU shall not live on credit cards. They should be used for emergency purposes only! This is not always the case for most people. Most people look at credit cards as another source of income—often to keep up their poor money management habits. Racking up credit card debt does not work in your favor. As a matter of fact, it hurts you in the long run. Credit cards should be used for gas, unavoidable travel expenses, or reasonable grocery purchases.

The reason why these purchases are advised, is because they are usually small purchases that can be paid off rather quickly or they fall within the percentile that lenders look at for spenders. Usually these purchases can be paid off within a 30-day cycle if you are properly operating within your budget.

Your credit cards must be organized. One way for them to be organized is to determine what they were acquired for. Why did you apply for the credit card? Credit card acquisitions can be either negative or positive. A positive use for a credit card is to help in building credit. A negative use of a credit card is using it as a cushion to continue spending poorly. Credit cards are never to be maxed out. Honestly, there is such a thing as over using your cards. This is an absolute turn off to lenders or investors.

When you use 30-35% of your credit cards' limit, it shows the lender that you are a responsible and intentional spender, not a careless one.

Pencil time! Fill in the blanks with your answers. Remember honesty is key.

1. Yes or No: Do you have a credit card?

2. Yes or No: Are any of your cards in collections?

3. I have _____ card(s).

4. _____ of my cards are in collections.

5. I use my card(s) approximately _____ times a month.

6. I use my credit card(s) to... _____

_____

_____

_____

Paying off credit card debt is not the hardest thing in the world to do, but it does take intentionality and consistency. Paying off the balance every month is a great achievement. You may not be able to pay off the balance right away. Paying off balances help with eliminating interest associated with the card. However, if you can't pay the balance, paying the minimum is absolutely okay. As you are starting this budget venture, you may not be able to regularly pay the balance. You can determine this based on what you wrote on your task list.

If you aren't able to pay off the balance due to lack of monies, it may have to carry over to the next pay cycle. But...and I repeat but—do not, *not* pay anything. Cover the minimum at the least and make sure the payment is on time. Paying credit card bills on time puts your financial picture in a positive light with creditors and lenders. It also puts you in a better position when you get ready to make those big purchases that was mentioned earlier.

You also need to eliminate unnecessary cards. Credit cards that are unmercenary are those that have no true benefits. Cards that provide points for hotels, airfare, car rentals, or restaurant rewards are beneficial cards to have. Reward points like those help you save money, and in return, keeps your financial picture growing strong.

If the credit cards that you have provide none of those things, it is time to get rid of them. I know that's a hard pill to swallow. Don't be sad–putting a budget in place will help you get those types of cards.

So, what are the benefits that come with your credit cards. There are seven segments for you to make your list. Hopefully you don't need more than that. If you do, chances are you have cards that need to be eliminated. Strive to eliminate the ones with the least benefits and the highest interest. Keep the two that are most beneficial. This will help you save money as well.

Credit Card List			
Card Name	Card Limit	Interest Rate	Benefit

Here is a strategy that you should use to pay off your credit card debt. Start your credit card payment regimen by paying the balance of the lowest bill first. The reason for this is because the money left over after you pay the lowest bill first can go towards the next card's balance. This will help you eliminate the credit card debt faster.

Here's an example: Below is a list of credit card balances

Capital One: $1789.00 minimum $57.00

American Express: $ 367.00 minimum $25.00

Discover: $829.00 minimum $47.00

Here is an example of how these should be paid:

Capital One: Pay the minimum $57.00

American Express: I pay $50.00

Discover: I pay $55.00

It should be noted that the first bill's balance was paid in full. The remaining monies were added to the other two cards balances.

I am able to lower the balance on the small card, which gives me the opportunity to pay it off quicker. Then a little extra money was put towards the Discover card to help reduce the balance and minimum on the highest card to make sure that it can be paid and in good standing. Then the money to pay on the American Express can be used. The $50.00 plus from the other minimum you were paying on Discover will then go towards lowering that bill. It works! You just have to be determined.

I know! I know! You're freaking out because you want to know where the extra money to pay these cards off are coming from. The extra money that generates after you complete your task list is how you can pay your credit card debt off. Yes, I do know that this same strategy was given to you for catching up on past due bills—that fact still remains.

If you go back to the beginning, you will notice that you were asked what your financial goals are. Hopefully you have eliminating credit card debt as one or catching up on bills as one. See which on you listed first. Chances are, the first one you listed is the one that is most important to you and should be tasked first. After you accomplish that, you can move on to the other.

SWIPER! NO SWIPING

"Don't swipe me, said no card ever!"

~Anonymous

WE'VE just learned about the importance of your credit card...how they're too be used, and how you are to be good stewards of them. So, now we're going to focus on the habit that causes most card carries to end up in past due statuses or maxing their limits. It's called the curse of the swipe!

Repeat after me— "swiper no swiping!" So, I'm going to have you say it again because I don't believe that you said it aloud the first time...and if you did, there's no harm in saying it again—swiper, no swiping! Swiper, absolutely, positively...no unnecessary, unplanned, spur of the moment, swiping!

Individuals that swipe their cards are chronic swipers. They're the type of people that swipe their cards so much that they don't even realize that they have no more money to spend. Chronic swipers are the ones at the register extending card number one, number two, number three-four-and five to the cashier in hopes that the total so that the spur of the moment purchase they are attempting to make would go through. Have you ever been at the grocery store and your total is, let's say $250...and you pull out your card knowing full well that you've only got $200 on it, and you swipe it anyway?

Shame on you! Can I just tell you, the bank is on the other side of that card waiting to approve it and slap an insufficient funds fee, and overdraft fee, and any other fee they can find to go along with it.

Pencil time! Let's find out where you are as far as chronic swiping. Answer the following questions by circling yes or no. Be honest!

1. Yes or No: Do you swipe your card for every purchase you make?

2. Yes or No: Is the bank taking money from you?

3. Yes or No: You tend to have overdraft fees due to insufficient funds?

4. Yes or No: Do you know that the fees associated with your account makes the bank and you lose money?

5. Yes or No: Do you withdraw money or over swipe because your check will be deposited with 24-48 hours?

If you've said yes to one of these questions, you have swipers' mentality, and again to you I say—swiper, no swiping! Card swiping should be planned. Now this is not to say that things don't happen, but if you're following the budget then an emergency swipe won't hurt. But everything is not, and I repeat, is not an emergency!

Now let's clarify something, because I can feel your anxiety even within these pages. Emergencies are not stress related emotional purchases. Nah! That type of swiping is known as stress swiping. Remember, we just discussed that there is a difference between a need and a want. Emotional spending to unwind, or calm down, or get over a situation is not a legitimate emergency. These type of chronic swipers simply swipe when the going gets tough or if the going gets amazing. They make every occasion a swipe-a-bration! Whenever anything drastic happens, you find something that you just have to swipe for—clothes, food, shoes. Chronic swiping puts you in debt.

Fear not! There are some swiper blocking strategies that will help curve your swiper habits. You can do it now, rather than later.

✓ Check your account balances daily!

✓ Only walk with a realistic amount of cash on hand for the week—this is determined by your task list.

✓ Live by the rule: when the cash is done for the week, then it is done!

✓ Make sure all bills are paid and cleared in your account before you make any additional withdraws or swipes.

MONEY LENDER

"Before borrowing money, decide which you need more—the person or the money."

~Q. Dynese

DON'T care who you are in life, and where you are in life—rich or struggling, we have all been guilty of lending money and borrowing money. Situations happen in life all the time where you or someone you know needs a quick loan, or a not so quick loan, or a quick loan that turns in to a not so quick pay back.

Time to write again. Answer the following questions by circling yes or no. Honesty is still the best policy, so be honest!

1. Yes or No: Have friends/family asked to loan money from you?

2. Yes or No: Do you have the money to lend outside of the funds set aside to take care of your task list?

3. Yes or No: Do you feel obligated to help when you're asked to loan money?

4. Yes or No: Can you afford to miss that money once you loan it out?

5. Yes or No: Are you capable of saying the word "no"?

6. Yes or No: Do you have a lending limit?

7. Yes or No: If the tables were flipped, would they loan it to you?

8. Yes or No: Have you asked to borrow money from friends/family?

9. Yes or No: Do you ask to borrow money often?

10. Yes or No: Do you have a payback plan?

These questions aren't to make you stop loaning money, or to even say that you are wrong for borrowing money at times. What these questions are designed to do is show you that there needs to be a clear line on how you borrow money from others, and how that money should be paid back; as well as, it should help define the line of when money is loaned from you and how it should be remitted.

There is a universal rule that is uttered in the lending and borrowing world, and that is: if you can't afford to miss it then you don't have it to loan out! Let's be honest, though some people that borrow money have every intention to pay it back–they don't, for whatever reason! I'm sure that there have been a few times that you've borrowed money that you didn't pay back or delayed in paying back for one reason or the other.

All is not lost—this money lending reality check comes with a tool that can help you get your money lending days in check. It's an agreement for you to get your money back. Before we get into that, let talk about those that shouldn't be on your lenders list for any reason. This is known as your black list. You need to draft this list. This is a list of those people that you will not lend money to under any circumstances.

Things to consider when creating this list: do they always need a loan? Do they pay you back? When they pay you back, is it on time? Does loaning money to him/her put you in a tight spot every time? If your answers are "yes" these individuals need to be black listed. Take the blank space below to jot down the names of those that are or need to be on your black list.

1. _____   6. _____

2. _____   7. _____

3. _____   8. _____

4. _____   9. _____

5. _____   10. _____

Now, the next thing to consider is this; you cannot be a hypocrite. Well, you can be a hypocrite, but you shouldn't be. If you are going to create a black list of your own, you should ensure that you are not on the black list of any of your friends or family. So, let's see where you are. Write a list of the family and friends that you owe, and the amounts that are to be paid back.

1. _____   6. _____

2. _____   7. _____

3. _____   8. _____

4. _____   9. _____

5. _____   10. _____

Sample Money Lender Agreement:

I (your name) agree to lend (lendees name) money in the amount of \$_____.
This amount is to be paid back on or before (Month Day, Year).

_____

Lender's Signature

_____

Lendee's Signature

Sample Money Lender Agreement with Interest:

I (your name) agree to lend (lendees name) money in the amount of \$_____.
This amount is to be paid back on or before (Month Day, Year). The aforementioned amount
will be paid back with the agreed upon interest of \$_____.

_____

Lender's Signature

_____

Lendee's Signature

EMERGENCY FUNDS

"Something is always coming along that will cost you money, so be prepared."
~Rachel Cruze

N THE chapters before we've harped on what an emergency is not! It should be so clear in your mind that you do not have to go over it again. So, with that being said, let's talk about emergency funds—how to establish it, and why they're important.

An emergency fund are monies set aside for unforeseen personal circumstances that affect you or your household financially. It's the survival mode safe. Circumstances that fall under this category are: car and home repairs, major medical expenses, unexpected emergency travel (bereavement), emergency pet care, money owed to IRS, job loss, future rent/mortgage. The steps to starting this fund are:

- ✓ Get all bills in a current status
- ✓ Designate one bank account to this fund with limited access—no mattresses
- ✓ Do not pull anything from this account for outside financial obligations
- ✓ Set up an auto deposit of $25.00 to start this fund

You may think that the $25.00 is such a small amount, but the object is not to have you making unrealistic deposits. These are small steps to your financial sanity. Any extra money after the task list is complete and debts are paid, should go to your emergency fund. Any money from your hustle should be split between your savings and emergency funds.

This is where your family should come into alignment. The house should be on one accord when it comes to budgeting. Why? How about the fact that everyone will be affected by the budget?

Who are those that are affected by your budget and who are those that affect your budget? Grab your pencil, and let's get to work. On the lines below, write the names of those in your household that will be affected by the budget. Even if they're renting a room or sleeping on the sofa. They're income, or non-income will affect the household cash flow.

MONETARY CONTRIBUTORS			
Cousin Braxton $275.00			
		TOTAL	

Here's a word of advice, don't just go crazy and cut everyone's allowances or money flow without having a conversation with them about what is about to take place and why. Having a conversation is crucial when creating and maintaining a budget. One reason for this is because you want everyone's buy in on what is about to go down, especially if you have children who have always helped you spend your money!

This is an excellent way to establish accountability partners. Once it is established that the budget is about to happen, try implementing a family financial picture board. It brings about team work, and helps everyone in the house know what it is that you're working towards. This board can be filled with words or pictures that project an upcoming vacation or staycation, a special occasion (birthday party, sweet sixteen), a home improvement goal, shopping, a car, college funds, purchasing a new house, etc.

This vision board also helps savings to accrue faster. With everyone knowing that the family is on a mission, it strikes a chord for everyone to begin reigning in their spending. Make sure that this vision board has plenty of pictures. Pictures stimulate the cortex of the brain, and gives the onlooker a visual to achieve.

SAVINGS WORK

"Small forced savings every month will lead to huge magical returns."

~Nirmal Jain

SAVINGS! This word has been mentioned several times within this workbook. Saving takes intentionality and discipline. It is the money you set aside just in case of a minor unforeseen circumstance. It is different from an emergency fund; however, an emergency fund can be classified as a type of savings.

Pencil time! Answer the following questions by circling yes or no. By now you should know that honesty is key.

1. Yes or No: Do you have a savings account?

2. Yes or No: Do you have a bank account at all?

Short Answer Response:

3. The money in my savings account comes from: _____

_____

_____

_____

_____

4. How many bank accounts do you have? _____

If you don't have a savings account, I encourage you to get one. The extra monies that come in from your hustle/business, and that is left over after you take care of your financial task list is what needs to be deposited into your savings account.

Savings are important because everything you do in the future should be planned for financially. For example, if you're planning for a family vacay, you need to establish a savings for that. I hear your thoughts. You're sitting there wondering why. Well, here it is! Everything that you do while on vacation will deplete your daily, weekly, and monthly income, so why not give it its own cash flow. The hotel, car, activities, food, etc. that you will be shelling money out for during your time should be projected and written out. By doing this, you have a greater chance of not overspending on vacation. You'll also be able to see if you are in a position financially to take the vacation.

Another form of a savings fund is a holiday budget. No matter how far in advance we plan, the holidays seem to rush around the corner as if it never left. You should establish a holiday budget. Thanksgiving, Christmas, and New Year's tend to stress everyone out because of the financial burden it brings. It usually brings about a burden because people under plan and over spend for all of these seasons. Just because sales are everywhere doesn't mean that you have extra money to spend. It simply means that you have quicker ways to spend the money that you've saved.

Non-budgeters tend to stress about savings because they try to save large amounts at a time. But $5, $10, $15 is enough to start a savings. If you can do more (your task list will tell you if you can) then do more, but whatever you do, start on your level. Your savings is the account that you can borrow from (instead of family/friends) when you need extra help. That money is then to be repaid with as much gusto as you would if it were from someone else.

You should also review your savings account every pay cycle—not every day. Upon your first review, you should set saving goals. Every quarter you should set a certain amount that you want to save. Multiple accounts are great to establish when considering savings. It helps you to keep better track of your money. Checking, savings household bills, and emergency funds are the accounts that should be established. These don't have to be at multiple banks. You can set them up under one bank.

If you want to be more anal on establishing your savings account, you can set up your holiday and vacation accounts separately from your regular savings. Again, this is a suggestion not a mandate. It is pretty drastic, but hey! Drastic times call for drastic measures.

Speaking of measures—let's talk PII (pronounced pie) but not to be confused with a slice of dessert. With that being said, your priorities, integrity, and intentions is what makes PII. Everyone should live by this minimal slogan. It is a way to ensure optimal financial success.

So what is PII exactly? It is a method that can be used for personal or business finances. First you start with priorities. In this instance, your priorities are your ways of producing or gaining income. Your integrity is focused on who you pay/owe to maintain the business or home. Your intentions, now those are your goals—what you're saving towards your goals, whether it's business expansion or household goals.

TESTIMONIALS

"There's no testimony without the test."
~Dr. Travis C. Jennings

Client 1# D. Taylor – my testimony while working with Angela has been that of a fresh start. Before working with Angela, I was in a terrible state of mind when it came to spending and handling money. I wasn't tithing like I was supposed to. Angela was quick to point all of this out. Now my mindset is that of saving and preparing for future and tithing correctly, and even though to tithe correctly meant going up on how much I had been giving previously, I now see more money than I had before I made that correction in my tithes. Working with Angela has made me more self-aware of former bad habits such as spending what I don't have, and over-drafting my account. She has been an accountability partner like none other in keeping me in line with the system we have set up and I thank God for her.

Client 2# T. Martinez – I have been working with Angela since I was in college and I must say that she has definitely helped me develop a greater level of discipline with my finances. She's taught me how to allocate my funds in a very responsible manner. Since using her, I have been able to purchase my first home, a new car and travel internationally, without feeling strained. I now have my regular checking account, an account for my housing expenses and an emergency account. I have been able to save thousands as a result!

Client 3# A. Malcolm - my overall experience with the budget administrator was absolutely amazing. The ability to be able to not only save money for my goals and desires but to get long lasting wisdom on my finances as whole is invaluable. During the 8-9 months I worked with the budget administrator, I was able to save over $2500 and pay all my bills on time. I was even able to take a trip to Cape Town South Africa and not feel anxious about bills when I returned home.

Client 4# M. Peterson – I am a single mom of a teen girl and young boy! I began working with Angela, March of 2018. My budget experience was very eye opening. When we began, she gathered all of my information (debt, expense, etc.) she discovered I had false burdens and helped me to transition from that. Angela then addressed how I was spending money from different accounts with no real structure and she helped me organize how to spend from the correct accounts. She involved my kids and they were absolutely excited to be apart! It is funny how they care about spending from their own money and have no regard for spending mine—LOL. They now think before spending! I also like how she included them in the household budget so that they could see and understand how all incoming income was being allocated. Our overall experience gave us nuggets to be financially sober and stable. Angela Francis we thank you and keep up the great work.

Client #5 K. French – As a new resident to Georgia, and a single parent, I had a lot financial pressure. Money had always made me nervous. Angela not only helped me understand the importance of my credit score, but she helped me manage my money. I was able to buy a house within a few months. I was able keep to my child in private school. I have been able to look at finances without stress and rely on what she has taught me. Angela helped me change my view on budgeting. I no longer look at it as an enemy, but as a buddy.

Client #6 J. Laster - Angela has helped me manage my bills. Her service is awesome. She was able to get my finances on the straight and narrow. My bills have been paid on time since working with her. She always communicates with me monthly concerning my finances. I travel a lot for work and I am not able to log on or write a check to pay my bills with my busy schedule. Before meeting Angela, I forgot to pay bills not due to lack of money, but due to lack of time management. Now I don't get any past due notices or calls from merchants because she takes care of it for me monthly using the funds I've learned to save in my accounts.

NOTES

CPSIA information can be obtained
at www.ICGtesting.com
Printed in the USA
LVHW102118300119
605868LV00001B/7/P